A Little book of Big
CORNISH
ACHIEVEMENTS

Published by Atmosphere
Willis Vean
Mullion Cornwall TR12 7DF
England
Tel 01326 240180

Text Copyright 2007 by Liz Mitchell and Diane Sexton
All images Copyright 2007 by Bob Croxford
Book Design and typography by Bob Croxford Copyright Atmosphere 2007
Printed and bound in Italy

ISBN 978-0-9550805-0-0

Cover: A replica of Trevithick's 'Puffing Devil' built by The Trevithick Society against a background of the Eden Project's Biomes

CONTENTS

INTRODUCTION

Cornwall was a small remote county with a small population and yet contributed much to the world. Few realise that in Stone Age times the land which is now Cornwall was the most densely populated area in Britain witnessed by the large number of megalithic sites. Lately doubt has been cast on the belief that the original dwellers were a Celtic race. Some theories now suggests that the inhabitants long ago were a separate and distinct tribe who sensibly kept clear of the warring Mercians and Saxons and therefore never entered the history books.

Little changed for the Cornish until the Bronze Age, when metal craft came into being and Cornwall acquired significance as a supplier of tin and copper, forging and establishing trading links with other nations.

For much of their early history, the people of Cornwall were poor and with low prospects. With bad roads and fertile land reduced by large areas of granite outcrops, the county had little in its favour. What little Cornwall had, was to be found deep underground.

After trading in minerals for thousands of years in a very small way, the 18th Century was to bring a massive change.

Mechanisation was to increase the yield from the mines and create the first steps in the Industrial Revolution. But for the lack of coal Cornwall would have continued as the centre of the Industrial Revolution, but because of the cost involved bringing coal into the county, the heart of the industrial development moved to the Midlands, but this did not deter the inventive spirit. Almost like the blooming of a flower, the seed of Cornish ingenuity burst forth and the county became a hotbed of innovation. The contribution to progress made by Cornish engineers resulting from the mining industry, led to the development of the world's first motorised car for example, and because of the county's geographic location;

the world's first transatlantic wireless communication.

Cornwall has spawned its fair share of pioneers both in medical sciences and geographical exploration.

The county can bask in the glory of three Nobel Prize winners which, on a 'per capita' basis puts Cornwall ahead of all other countries.

The fact that Cornwall is a peninsula lends itself to the leisure pursuits of sailing and surfing both of which flourish. The traditional farming and fishing industries continue to survive despite the multi-faceted layers of bureaucracy placed upon them. Currently there are many organizations working together to ensure that fishing stocks are maintained and preserved for future generations. The farming industry is diversifying to accommodate climate change and embracing tourism, to ensure its survival.

Tourism has always been part of the Cornish economy and never more so than now, offering the modern day tourist a wide choice of attractions comparable to other destinations, but for those who are looking for peace and tranquillity there are still plenty of quiet corners to sit and nourish the soul. The mere fact that the pace is slow has allowed for the nurture of the creative spirit, which in turn has produced many famous artists and writers. Film makers from around the world have been drawn to the county for its temperate climate and dramatic scenery since the 1920's. It has been our intention to provide the reader with sufficient information to surprise, enlighten and entertain. We have tried to include as broad a spectrum of achievements, and to reveal to the wider world the skills, creative genius and idiosyncrasies of both the Cornish and people and events associated with the county of Cornwall, as befits the size of this book.

First Tourist

Pytheas of Massillia, a Greek, was the first tourist to visit St. Michael's Mount. He named Cornwall Belerion, meaning the Shining Land in 4th century BC, and it was the first place to be named in the British Isles. Present day mariners say that the land, viewed from the sea does appear to shine particularly after a shower of rain, but it was probably the tin Pytheas was referring to. He was very impressed by the way the indigenous peoples mined the tin and copper from the ground, and found them to be a cultured and refined society, which he attributed to their trading links with people from around the world.

First Cross Country Postal System

Ralph Allen, a real trail-blazer, was born in 1694 at St Blazey Highway in Cornwall. He instigated the first cross-country postal system, which improved the postal service for England and Wales; amassing a personal fortune of half a million pounds along the way. This enabled him to buy quarries at Combe Down, from which he in turn supplied the stone that built some of the finest houses in Bath. In 1742 he went on to become Mayor of that city.

First Australian Convict Ship

Launceston man James Ruse was convicted of burglary having stolen two silver watches valued at five pounds. His death sentence was commuted to deportation on the first Australian convict ship, the Scarborough, in 1787. On arrival in Australia, supplies were low, and Ruse was allocated several acres of cleared land in which to provide food for the colony. He was successful and when his sentence expired in 1792, the title of this land was deeded to him; the first land grant in the colony. He went from dishonour to honour when his work in farming resulted in agricultural colleges being named after him. All in all, a good ruse!

First Blood Donor Service

The concept for the first voluntary blood donor service was devised by St Ives born Percy Lane Oliver in 1921.

St Michael's Mount

First Author to Sell a Million Books in his Lifetime

Silas Hocking 1850-1935, born at St-Stephen-in-Brannel was a minister in the United Methodist Free Church, but later turned his ability to writing fiction. He was reputed to have been the first writer to ever sell a million copies of his books in his lifetime. Books included were "His Father: Or A Mother's Legacy" and "Her Benny."

First International Mail Service

In 1689 the ocean-going Mail Packet Ships established the first international mail service between Falmouth and Corunna in Spain. In 1702 the service crossed the Atlantic to the West Indies. De Wynn's Coffee House in Falmouth is where captains of the Packet Ships would congregate to receive their orders.

First Blood Transfusion

Richard Lower born at St Tudy near Bodmin in 1631, studied medicine and established a practice in London. He went on to become a Fellow of the Royal Society in 1667. He was the first person to perform an operation of blood transfusion direct from one vein of a dog into the vein of another and finally from man to man. He became physician to Charles II.

First Arab Horse

The first Arab horse was brought to England from France by the second Earl of Godolphin of the Goldophin Estate near Helston, and was known as the Godolphin Arabian. The King, Louis XIV of France declined the stallion which had previously been offered to him as a gift. It is reputed the horse had once pulled a water cart in the streets of Paris. From such low beginnings he went on to become one of the three race horses, from which all thoroughbred racehorses throughout the world descend. His faithful stable companion was a cat called Grimalkin.

De Wynn's Coffee House

First Helicopter Service

The first scheduled helicopter service in Europe was launched in 1964 transporting passengers between Penzance and the Isles of Scilly. It has now become the oldest helicopter passenger service in the world.

First Steam Rock Boring Machine

In 1812 Harvey's of Hayle built the world's first steam-powered rock boring machine. The company also built Cornish beam engines and other equipment relating to mining, many of these items were exported world-wide.

First Air to Ground Message

In 1920, Cornishman Donald Healey, perhaps better known for his association with motor cars and motor racing transmitted the first air-to-ground radio message over Perranporth; the first possibly in the country.

First Radio Station

Garras Wharf, Truro is the home to the BBC's first purpose-built radio station which opened in 1982.

Isles of Scilly Helicopter Service

First Transatlantic Radio Signal

Standing on the cliffs at Poldhu near Mullion, looking out over the vast stretch of water, it is hard to grasp that this was the point from which transatlantic wireless communication began. It is the Italian inventor Guglielmo Marconi, born in 1874 to whom we must pay homage. It was on the 12th of December 1901, that the faint signal for the letter 'S' transmitted from the wireless station at Poldhu was picked up by an aerial on Signal Hill in Newfoundland, some 2,700km (1,700mls) away. Today we can stand on the same spot and text messages via our mobile phones across the globe, and use the internet etc, with ease; all because Marconi believed and proved that wireless communications over long distances by electromagnetic waves was possible, and that they were not prevented by the earth's curvature.

First Manned Flight

Farmer Richard Pearse emigrated from Cornwall to New Zealand. His construction of a plane made from bamboo, wire and canvas is reputed to be the first aeroplane to fly in public; eight months before the Wright Brother's in December 1903. The plane and its inventor, Richard Pearse are subjects of a special exhibition at Flambards, near Helston.

First Harvest Festival

Reverend Hawker of Morwenstowe began his rectorship in 1834 and is believed to be the first vicar to have preached in that parish for over one hundred years. His poem 'Song of the Western Men' was to become Cornwall's National Anthem. Hawker's lasting achievement was to introduce the idea of the Harvest Festival Service.

Monument to Marconi's first Transatlantic Radio Signal

First Polytechnic

The word polytechnic was first introduced into the English language in 1833 having been invented by Caroline Were Fox at the age of fourteen. The first polytechnic was opened in Church Street Falmouth in the same year, and Caroline was the last survivor of those who attended the opening meeting. From an early age Caroline mixed with the academic elite; her father being Robert Were Fox. She devoted her efforts to making education available to the masses. The Falmouth Polytechnic was successfully up and running five years before Quintin Hogg's polytechnic in Regent Street

First Compulsory Education

There's nothing silly about the Isles of Scilly! Augustus Smith introduced compulsory education in 1834, some thirty years before it was introduced on the mainland.

First Smoke

Tobacco was introduced into English society in 1586 by Sir Walter Raleigh and the plant in Elizabethan times was known as sotweed. Sir Walter is reputed to have smoked his first tobacco in public as a guest of the Killigrew's at Falmouth.

Falmouth's First Custom House

The Killigrew family of Arwenack Manor built the first Custom House and the King's Pipe; a large chimney. The former was to collect the revenue from imported goods and the latter to burn any illegally imported tobacco.

The King's Pipe

First Air Ambulance

The UK saw the first air ambulance service launched in Cornwall on the first of April 1987. With Cornwall's tight network of country lanes, the air ambulance has been an invaluable lifesaver, transporting upwards of 12,000 people during this period. It relies solely on voluntary contributions by the general public. Long may it continue!

Photo: John Callan

Cornwall's Air Ambulance

First Commercial Wind Farm

In 1991 Cornwall was instrumental in setting up the the first commercial windfarm at Delabole, promoting green energy. Although not loved by everyone from a visual perspective, the ten turbines have an annual output of approximately 12,000,000 Kw hours, subject to wind speeds, equalling 1 year's consumption by 2,700 average homes. There are seven wind farms in Cornwall, of which Delabole is the smallest, all helping to reduce the effect of greenhouse gases.

Delabole Windfarm

First Duke of Cornwall

Edward, first Duke of Cornwall was the eldest son of Edward III, and subsequent eldest sons of the Monarchy have been given this title from birth. Both he and his father were able military commanders, the Prince having won his spurs at the Battle of Crecy at the age of sixteen in 1346. He went on to victory winning several battles in the Hundred Years War, and became known as the Black Prince because of the colour of his armour. In 1347 Fowey supplied forty seven ships, which was more than any other town in England, for the seige of Calais.

First Census

Charles Abbot MP for Helston in 1798, was infuriated by the absence of official records for Parliamentary proceedings, and took measures to make Parliamentary decisions more accessible. He was responsible for the first census act in 1799.

First Inch to a Mile Map

It was in 1699 that Joel Gascoyne produced the first inch to a mile map in Britain and the first county mapped was Cornwall.

First Public Road Race

The Pendennis Castle road races were the first motorcycle races run on public roads in Britain. They were held between 1931 and 1937. G E Rowley of Sidcup held the lap record for the 1.5 mile course at 1min. 44 seconds.

Pendennis Race Track

Oldest Bridge

Yeolm Bridge is the oldest and best finished bridge in Cornwall. It dates back to the 14th century having two pointed arches with supporting ribs. The ribs which are chamfered closely resemble the arch of the North Gate at Launceston Castle.

Yeolm Bridge

Oldest Slate Quarry

Delabole Slate Quarry is the oldest working slate quarry in England. Its building material has been used for well over six hundred years. It has been quarried continuously since the early 17th century. It is 425 feet deep and more than a mile and a half in circumference.

Oldest Manor

Penfound Manor is the oldest inhabited manor house in Britain. It was mentioned in the Domesday Book and is reputed to be haunted. This unique property is open to the public.

Oldest Museum

The Wayside Museum at Zennor covers all aspects of domestic and working life, with over five thousand items in fifteen display areas. It is the oldest privately owned museum in Cornwall.

Oldest Shipping Company

Fox's Shipping Agency in Falmouth is probably the oldest in the world, it was founded in 1646.

Oldest Brew Pub

The Blue Anchor in Coinagehall Street, Helston is the oldest brewery in Cornwall and the oldest brewery in the country which still brews ale on the premises. It became an inn during the fifteenth century and the ale it produces known as Spingo, is renowned for its potency.

The Blue Anchor

Oldest Charter Town

Marazion is the oldest Charter Town in Cornwall having received its charter in 1257 during the reign of King Henry III.

Oldest Pre-pendulum Clock

The oldest known domestic pre-pendulum clock dating back to the 1500s is to be found in the chapel at Cotehele House near Calstock.

Oldest Oratory

St Piran's Oratory is probably the oldest chapel in Cornwall and is thought to date back to the 7th century. It was dedicated to the Cornish Saint, St Piran, but sadly the remains of this little chapel have been consumed by sand.

Oldest Beam Engine

Driven by steam, the oldest restored beam engine in the country is to be found at the famous cliff edge Levant Mine.

Oldest Settlement

Carn Brea has the remains of the oldest and largest human settlement in Cornwall. It is a 46 acre hill fort with far reaching views covering most of West Cornwall.

Carn Brea

First Car

Cornish genius Richard Trevithick was born on the 13th April 1771 and it was he who constructed the first motor car. Designed to run on the road it was the first self propelled vehicle run by a high pressure steam engine. The first full size engine had its test run going up Camborne Hill on Christmas Eve 1801. The following day his vehicle took to the roads again causing great excitement, and alarm to some as it drove through the centre of Camborne, gaining the nickname of The Puffing Devil. He is accredited with inventing steam threshers, stamps and rock boring machines along with surface condensers and the first central heating systems for rooms. He went to Peru for eleven years, leaving wife and family behind; the main purpose was to use his invention to pump out silver mines. Whilst in Peru he made money from his steam engines which enabled him to buy his own silver mines. After war broke out in Peru in 1826 Trevithick beat a hasty retreat to Costa Rica then on to Columbia. Having lost all his money he was lent the fare home by the engineer Robert Stephenson who was building a railway there.

Puffing Devil Replica

Pears Soap

Andrew Pears of Mevagissey trained as a barber and in 1812 was founder of the Pears Soap Company. The soap he produced was not only of the highest quality, but it was almost transparent and sold for the princely sum of one shilling and half a crown respectively. Andrew, fearing imitations went so far as to sign every package sold.

Pear's Soap

Inventor of the Double Cylinder Engine

In 1781 Jonathan Hornblower invented the double cylinder engine described as a machine engine for raising water and other liquids by means of fire and steam.

Inventor of Gaslighting

1792 William Murdoch commenced experiments at his home in Redruth on the illuminating properties of gases produced by distilling coal, wood and peat creating the first usable amounts of gas. The house, which can still be seen, was the first house to be lit by gas.

First Gaslit House

Safety Fuse

In 1831, Cornish resident William Bickford invented the safety fuse. The increase of accidents that occurred 'shooting the rocks' by the crude way in which the gun-powder was ignited to break up the rock face, caused Bickford immense concern. Visiting a retired ropemaker friend, he saw how the yarns were spun, and the idea of pouring gunpowder from a funnel into the centre of the rope as it was spun, and then sealing it, resulted in the Bickford Fuse. It saved thousands of lives, but some miners and quarrymen reverted back to the old method because they had to purchase the fuses, and many could not afford to do so

Inventor of Man Engine

Michael Loam invented the Man Engine in 1834 winning a prize offered by the Royal Cornwall Polytechnic Society. His invention was first erected in 1842 at Tresavean Mine, Gwennap to a depth of 45 metres and was powered by a water wheel. The miners stepped on platforms from one rod to the other alternately. In 1843 the depth was extended to 530 metres and was powered by a 36 inch engine. To emphasise its safety, school children were taken down to a hundred fathoms. Nevertheless there were fatal accidents; the first on the 31st September 1843 when a fourteen year old miner made a false step and fell twenty eight fathoms.

Inventor of Nitrous Oxide

Humphrey Davy, born in Penzance in 1778, served as an apothecary's apprentice. Having moved to Bristol he worked in researching the medical uses of gases. Extending his research of nitrous oxide through self experimentation as well as on his friends, the poets Coleridge and Southey. In 1807 Davy went on to discover potassium and sodium and his innovations led to the discovery of chlorine as a bleaching agent. In 1815 he invented the miner's safety lamp; its flame is enclosed by wire gauze and is commonly known as the Davy Lamp. At the age of twenty-three he became assistant lecturer at the Royal Institute London on the salary of one-hundred pounds per annum. He continued his experiments which included the electric arc lamp and Crookes Tube which we know today as x-rays. Nitrous Oxide has recently become popular as a clubland drug.

Humphrey Davy

Inventor of the 'Bude' Light

Goldsworthy Gurney was born at Treator near Padstow in 1793. He started his career in medicine but was more interested in science. He patented the Bude Light in 1838; a system of flashing lights whereby the number of flashes per minute would determine a particular lighthouse. He was knighted in 1863 for adapting the Gurney Stove for the heating, lighting and ventilation of the old House of Commons. He also made the first and longest journey in the world by a steam vehicle at sustained speed, when his steam engine travelled from Bath to London. To prove it could be done he built Bude Castle on sand using a concrete raft. In spite of his brilliance and many inventions he died penniless.

The Rocket Line Apparatus

After witnessing the sinking of HMS Anson at Loe Bar near Porthleven in December 1807, Henry Trengrouse, a Helston cabinet maker, was inspired to invent the Rocket Powered Rescue System. The Society of Arts granted him thirty pounds and rewarded him with a silver medal. Alexander I of Russia was so impressed with Trengrouse's invention when he saw it being used in the Baltic seas, that he invited him to Russia, offering full financial backing and assistance to develop his system; being a patriot Henry declined. The British Government ordered twenty of the apparatus but on examination decided they could easily produce it; compensating Trengrouse with a mere fifty pounds for his invention. His apparatus saved thousands of lives from shipwrecks worldwide and was later known as the Breeches Buoy.

Inventor of The Bath Oliver

William Oliver was born at Trevarno, nr Helston in 1695. Doctor Oliver as he later became known, practised as a physician and introduced the smallpox vaccine in 1724. He moved to Bath where he went on to invent the Bath Oliver Biscuit; a less fattening biscuit than its predecessor; the sweet Bath Oliver Bun.

Inventor of the Inclined Plane System

Cornish engineer, John Edyvean invented the inclined plane system in 1776 for use in canals avoiding the necessity for locks. An inclined plane is a system used on some canals for raising boats between different water levels. A sloping plane is used as a means of supporting part of a load reducing the force needed to raise it. This is similar to the principal used on specialist funicular railways.

Bath Oliver Biscuits

Largest Earth Station

Goonhilly Earth Station, positioned on the Lizard Peninsula is the largest Satellite station in the world. In July 1962 the first aerial was ready for the launch of Telstar. Arthur, the largest of the dishes has been given a listed building status. It has a purpose built multi-media centre and the site affords protection for a diversity of wildlife.

Goonhilly Earth Station

Largest Submarine Telegraph Station

An underground museum at Porthcurno reveals the story of when it was home to the largest submarine telegraph station in the world during the second world war.

Largest Water Wheel

Wheal Martyn, St Austell, boasts the largest working water wheel in Cornwall. The 35ft water wheel was originally used to pump clay slurry from the pit; it has a pitch back wheel. Made at Charlestown Foundry in the early 1880s, it stopped working around 1940 but was restored to working order in 1976.

Loe Pool

Largest Freshwater Lake

Near Porthleven is Loe Bar Pool, the largest freshwater lake in Cornwall and Loe Bar which separates the lake from the sea.

Largest block of granite

In 1902 a single block of granite was dislodged in one piece from the Polkanugga Quarry. It weighed around 2738 tons and 70 men climbed on to it to help record the event.

Pendennis Castle

Largest Castle

Pendennis Castle is the largest castle in Cornwall.

Largest Helicopter Base

Culdrose is one of the largest helicopter operating bases in Europe. It has a workforce of about 2,000 service and 1,000 civilian personnel. It is Cornwall's biggest single site employer - about 1.5% of the county's workforce. Including its satellite airfield on the Lizard it comprises a total area of 1512acres.

Largest Restoration Programme

The Lost Gardens of Heligan near Mevagissey has the largest garden restoration programme covering over 80 acres of pleasure and productive gardens. It is Britain's only living museum of 19th century horticulture.

Largest Coastguard Station

The Maritime Rescue Co-ordination Centre, Falmouth is the largest and busiest, responsible for over half of the whole UK Search and Rescue Region, covering a sea area of some 660,000 square miles and a coastline of 250 miles. From someone cut off by the tide on a Cornish beach to a ship sinking in the Indian Ocean the MRCC co-ordinates all services. RNLI Lifeboats, R.A.F, RN and Coastguard helicopters, Coastguard Rescue Teams and beach lifeguards, to mention but a few. The Ops. room is packed with state of the art satellite and terrestrial communications equipment and is manned 365 days of the year. In 2005 Falmouth dealt with 1,685 incidents, rendered assistance in 237 cases, 290 people received help and 12 hoax calls.

Falmouth Coastguard

Largest Cycling Museum

There may be nine million bicycles in Beijing, not quite as many bicycles can be found at the Old Station Camelford; home to Cornwall's and Britain's largest cycling museum. Over four hundred examples of cycles, the first cycle oil lamp, and an eclectic mix of objects, fobs and badges, connected with the history of cycling from 1818, are on display. An extensive library of related books and an old cycle repair shop are among many of the attractions. Cycling is not just a thing of the past. With the advent of popular cycling routes we can all get on our bikes.

Largest Man

Antony Payne, known as the Cornish Giant was born at Stratton near Bude. Standing at over seven feet tall he fought in the battle of Stamford with his master Sir Bevil Grenville.

The Biomes at Eden Project

Largest Greenhouse

Near St Austell is Eden; the world's largest greenhouse. The enormous biomes were erected in a disused clay pit and in spring 2001 the Eden Project was opened to the public; the whole centre has become an environmental showcase. The two geodesic conservatories house some of the planets most exotic plants ranging from those found in the tropical rainforests, to the more temperate climate of the Mediterranean.

Largest Oil Slick

March 18th 1967 saw the world's largest ever oil slick. The Torrey Canyon cargo ship was carrying 119,328 tons of crude oil when it ran aground on the Seven Stones Reef off the coast of Cornwall. Three days later the slick was 35 by 20 miles. The impact on the environment was devastating polluting the coast, north and south. Even after 40 years it remains the 12th biggest oil spill ever known.

Smallest Town

St Just near Lands End is the smallest town in Cornwall; its inhabitants amount to approximately 3,800. Another point to ponder is that it is the furthest town away from a motorway in England.

Smallest Royal Dockyard

The village of Mylor was once the site of the smallest Royal dockyard in Britain; today it is still a very busy yachting harbour.

Smallest Gaol

At St Tudy near Wadebridge you can find the smallest gaol in Cornwall; it is affectionately known to the locals as the Clink. Luckily it is no longer used.

St Just

St Tudy Clink

Smallest Watch

John Arnold, Bodmin born in 1744 was to become one of the most famous clockmakers of London. In 1764 he made the smallest repeating watch and gave it as a birthday gift to George III who wore it set in a ring on his finger. He also made a chronometer which Captain Cooke used on his voyages to help him with navigation.

Smallest Methodist Preaching Place

In the village of Trewint is Wesley Cottage where John Wesley, the founder of Methodism, preached and rested. A two room extension was purpose built by the stonemason Digory Isbell who owned the cottage. The rooms are believed to be the smallest Methodist preaching place in the world and there is an annual Wesley Day celebration held there in May.

Smallest Shop

In the picturesque fishing village of Polperro there are premises which are reputed to be the smallest shop in England. Its dimensions are 5ft 6ins × 6ft or 1.68m ×1.83m.

Smallest Shop

Trewint Preaching Place

First Explorers to Discover the Source of the River Niger

Brothers Richard and John Lander were born at the 'Fighting Cocks' Inn in Truro in 1804 and 1807 respectively. In 1830 they went to Africa and became the first to discover the source of The River Niger. Richard was the first to receive The Royal Geographical Society's Medal and later returned to Africa in 1832 where he died from gunshot wounds at Fernando Po.

Discovery of Tahiti

Cornishman Samuel Wallis took command of HMS Dolphin in 1766. His brief was to explore the Pacific Ocean for land. Almost one year later he discovered Tahiti.

Lander Monument

First Discovery of Planet Neptune

John Couch Adams was born at Laneast near Launceston in 1819. He entered St John's College Cambridge at the age of twenty. The announcement of his discovery, by calculation only, of the remote planet of Neptune, gave him an international reputation as an astronomer and mathematician; forwarding his results to The Royal Observatory in Greenwich in 1845. The publication of his work was hindered by the attitude of his superiors. There was a public outcry when the French astronomer Leverrier, working independently received public acclaim when he managed to publish his papers on the subject ahead of Couch Adams.

DISCOVERIES

First Discovery of Manaccanite

In 1790 a far reaching discovery was made by William Gregor in a stream at Manaccan. He discovered a grey metallic element that we now know as Titanium. Previously called manaccanite and gregorite, it is used in space flight because of its strength and weight, but also because of its high resistance to corrosion. It has proved invaluable in surgical joint replacement and dentistry.

First to Discover that Heat Increases with Depth and the Dipping Needle

Robert Were Fox was born in Falmouth in 1789 and studied the internal temperature of the earth. He was first to discover that heat increases with depth but in a diminishing ratio. His interest in magnetism led to his invention of the dipping needle, which was used as an aid to explorers in Arctic seas in the study of magnetic phenomena.

The Chemiosmotic Hypothesis

Peter D Mitchell proposed the chemiosmotic hypothesis in 1961. This was considered a radical idea at the time, and was not universally accepted. Eventually the weight of evidence moved in his favour and he was awarded the Nobel Prize for Chemistry in 1978. From 1963 he oversaw the restoration of Glynn House near Bodmin Moor with his assistant Jennifer Moyle, part of which became a private laboratory.

Discovery of Pulsars

Anthony Hewish born in Fowey in 1924 was awarded a Nobel Prize in 1974 for his decisive role in the discovery of pulsars; a new classification of stars.

Site of the discovery Titanium

Only 'Quickie' Marriage Church

St Catherine's Church at Temple founded in the 12th century by the Knights Templar was the only church entitled to perform quickie marriages without Banns or Licence. It could have been a blessing in disguise for any young maiden who had fallen from grace; the Gretna Green of Cornwall.

Only Clifftop Theatre

Porthcurno is the setting for Minack, the magnificent Romanesque amphitheatre. Built into the side of granite cliffs, the idea came from the imagination of the late Miss Rowena Cade in the 1930s. The theatre is a popular venue for Shakespearian plays, comedies and musicals throughout the summer months.

Minack Theatre

Temple Church

Only Octogenarian to Walk to London

On hearing the news of the Great Exhibition of 1851, Mary Kelynack aged 84 years decided she would walk from her home at Madron in Cornwall to the Metropolis. Not only did Mary walk the three-hundred miles, she was received by the Lord Mayor who gave her a sovereign, had tea with the Lady Mayoress in the Mansion House, and was presented to Queen Victoria and Prince Albert at the exhibition. It took Mary five weeks to do the walk and she returned home safely to live another four years.

48 Waterwheels

It is difficult to imagine the hive of industry on the banks of the River Kennall at Ponsanooth during the 18th and 19th centuries. It was the only river in Cornwall and probably England to have forty-eight working water wheels in a seven mile stretch. The diverse industries ranged from corn milling to the production of paper, cloth and gunpowder to name but a few.

Only Race Circuit

Motor racing first took place on 9th August 1952 on a 2.6 mile circuit at Davidstow on Bodmin Moor. By 1953 the track had been reduced to 1.85 miles or 3.0km. It hosted Cornwall's sole Formula One race meetings until 1955. Sadly constant bad weather conditions contributed to its demise; rally events which still take place at Davidstow suffer the same problems.

Truro

Only City

The name of Truro is meant to represent the three rivers that converge on the inland city; The Kenwyn, The Truro and The Allen. It is Cornwall's only city and in the 12th century there existed a castle on what is now The Courts of Justice.

Only Cape in England

Cape Cornwall is the only cape in England.

Cape Cornwall

Greatest Words: 'They Shall Grow Not Old'

These words are familiar to most of us and they are the fourth stanza of a poem called "For the Fallen." The poem was composed in 1914 shortly after the start of the First World War. Laurence Binyon wrote this now famous poem whilst sitting on the cliff headland between Pentire Point and The Rumps, during a family holiday at Polzeath. The breath-taking beauty of his surroundings inspired him. His poem is recited annually in services of Remembrance.

Greatest Navigational Feat

Born at St Tudy in 1754, Cornishman William Bligh, famous for The Mutiny on the Bounty, must be given credit for the greatest navigational feat. He travelled 4,000 miles from Tofua to Timor in an open boat using a sextant as his only navigational aid. As a young naval officer he was sent out to survey the Helford River, to which end he was mistakenly arrested on suspicion of being a French spy.

National Hero

Sir Walter Raleigh Gilbert, born in Bodmin, shares the distinction along with the Duke of Wellington of being the only person to have an army medal issued with his picture on it.

The Rumps

First Organised Protest.

In 1497 there was a Cornish uprising against taxes imposed on them by Henry VII for his war against the Scots. Michael Joseph the local blacksmith (An Gof) of St Keverne and Thomas Flamank a Bodmin lawyer, rallied locals and marched to London. Reaching Blackheath, they were no match for the King's army of ten thousand men who surrounded them; the Cornishmen were poorly armed, the battle was short and two-hundred Cornishmen were killed. Flamank and Joseph were captured and executed at Tyburn ten days later.

An Gof and Thomas Flamank

The First News of Trafalgar

In 1805, the first announcement in the country of the victory at the Battle of Trafalgar, and the death of Nelson was made by the Mayor of Penzance from the balcony of the Union Hotel. The news was relayed by schooner to local fishermen who carried the information to Penzance. The bells of Madron Church rang out the news. John Richard Lapontiere, courier of the official news rode in a post-chaise from Falmouth to London. This journey usually took one week by stagecoach, but Lapontiere's took only thirty-eight hours.

Only Civil War Battles on Cornish Soil.

On the 19th January 1643 a civil war battle was fought at Braddock Down. The other was at Stamford Hill near Stratton on the 16th May in the same year. The Roundheads won.

The Union Hotel

Largest Harbour

As the largest natural harbour in the country and the third largest in the world Falmouth played an important role during the Second World War. The natural harbour of Carrick Roads had more than one hundred vessels anchored there at any one time. It was said that it was possible to walk across the estuary by stepping from one boat to the next.

Largest Number of Telephones

The Smugglers Cottage. This charming cottage tucked away at Tolverne on the Roseland Peninsula was requisitioned by the Admiralty for the use of high ranking Americans. General Eisenhower visited the troops here in the build up to the D Day Landings. Thirteen telephone lines were installed in the cottage.

First Swing Wing Aircraft

Predannack Airfield was instrumental in the development of the supersonic swing winged Swallow and Goose aircraft project. Barnes Wallis, the aeronautical engineer used radio controlled models to prove the concept of a 'Swing Wing' aeroplane. Many modern day fighter planes such as the Tornado and B-1B Bomber's are swing wing aircraft.

Oldest Commanding Officer.

Pendennis Castle was the last Royalist stronghold in the Civil War; it held out until August 1646. Finally, the eighty year old Sir John Arundell, who was commander of the Royalists, marched out of the castle in a display of pageantry, which marked the end of the Civil War.

Falmouth Docks

MILITARY

First Bouncing Bomb

The Dam Buster. Guy Penrose Gibson, born in August 1918, spent his boyhood days in Porthleven. On 16th May 1943, he led the Dam Buster's raid, in which his squadron of Lancaster Bombers destroyed a number of dams in Germany. The planes each carried a single bouncing bomb which was invented by Barnes Wallis.

Lancaster Bomber

The Oldest Naval Disaster.

Roger Grenville of Kilkhampton, Cornwall was Captain of Henry VI-II's flagship The Mary Rose when it accidentally sank in The Solent. The King witnessed the event which resulted in the loss of 470 men.

First Air Station

Little evidence remains today of the site which was the home to Cornwall's first air station. Work began on the Lizard Air Ship Station, subsequently known as Royal Naval Air Station Mullion in June 1916. Built on land belonging to the Bonython Estate near Cury Cross Lanes, the station became the centre of airship operations in the South West. The airships were engaged in U-boat (submarine) searches, identifying their location to Royal Naval vessels by means of Wireless Telegraphy. As the war progressed it became vital to keep the Channel and the Western Approaches as safe as possible for civilian, merchant and Royal Naval ships from the U-boat menace. The airship patrols were long and arduous but the men who flew them were hardy individuals.

Greatest Wartime Raid

The modest memorial on Fish Strand Quay Falmouth records one of greatest military raids of the Second World War; 'Operation Chariot'. The combined operations of a 600 plus task force, including 150 commandos left Falmouth on 26th March 1942 with a secret mission to destroy the docks at St Nazaire in enemy occupied France. The mission was accomplished, but more than 160 lives were lost. Five Victoria Crosses were awarded in recognition of the bravery during the raid.

Operation Chariot Memorial

Highest Hill

Looming out of the rugged landscape of Bodmin Moor, vying for supremacy are two of the highest peaks in Cornwall. Rough Tor is just a mere sixty-four feet smaller than its larger neighbour Brown Willy, which at a height of 1,375 feet makes it the largest hill in Cornwall.

Largest Serpentine Rock

Kynance Cove has the largest outcrop of serpentine rock in Britain. This rock is unique to the Lizard Penninsula where craftsmen can be seen producing decorative objects.

Discovery of China Clay

Formerly known as kaolin and latterly china clay, this soft white substance was first discovered at Tregonning Hill near Helston by chemist William Cookworthy in the mid eighteenth century. The clay is to be found largely in granite rich areas for which Cornwall is renowned. This product has many beneficial uses, paper, toothpaste, talcum powder and medicinal, to name but a few, but most notable is its use in the manufacture of fine porcelain. Known locally as the Cornish Alps, the white mountainous waste tips still bear witness to the china clay industry.

Rough Tor

China Clay Mining

Longest Coastline

Being a peninsula county, Cornwall has the longest and most diverse coastline in Britain. Depending on how it is measured, headland to headland or water's edge, it is between three hundred miles and just over one thousand. From the rugged and dramatic cliffs of the North Coast to the gentle and perhaps more forgiving sandy beaches of the West. It is without doubt that the geology of the county has been moulded by the storm-lashed and relentless tide; an example of this can be seen at Mounts Bay, when at low tide the remains of a fossilised forest can be seen protruding from beneath the sand. The evidence is clear; collapsed caves such as the Lion's Den and the Devil's Frying Pan on the Lizard Peninsula are also indicative of the destructive effect nature is having on the Cornish landscape.

Oldest Working Quarry

De Lank Quarry is the oldest quarry in Cornwall and has a reputation for producing some of the finest granite in the world. Some of the stone hewn from it has been used for the building of Tower Bridge, and the late Diana Princess of Wales's memorial in Hyde Park. More recently the De Lank Quarry supplied a granite boulder of 167 tonne which sculptor Pete Randall-Page carved into the 70 tonne 'Seed' for The Eden Project in Cornwall.

Coastline near Land's End

Overview

It is difficult to summarize the requirements of the various levels of bureaucracy associated with the fishing industry. Currently the Cornish sea fishing industry has to adhere to the EU fishing regulations and rules placed on them by the British Government. Stocks need preserving and in order to do so, licences have to be purchased for commercial fishing. There has been a de-commissioning of fishing boats; quotas have been levied on the fishermen and a cut in the number of the days at sea have been imposed. Fishing has been an integral part of Cornish life, and the fishermen recognise the need to preserve stocks; although the present situation has caused a loss in revenue for many, they are willing to comply providing that the same rules apply across all the member states. Currently there are many organisations working together to ensure that fishing stocks are maintained and preserved for future generations.

First Tagging in Cornwall

Fishing by hand line has always been part of the Cornish tradition and a number of fishermen are returning to this method. Line fishing is proving lucrative because of the condition of the fish when landed and the traceability of the commodity. This is a sustainable method and there is no wasted by product, which is something that appeals to the public. Two of the species currently tagged are Sea Bass and Pollock and by keying the number on the tag into your computer you can get details of the port where landed and fisherman who caught it.

Sea Bass

Oldest Lobster

The oldest lobster in Cornwall currently resides at the Padstow Hatchery. It is estimated to be fifty years old and is known affectionately as 'Dai The Claw'. In the wild a lobster can live up to one hundred years, but in order to do so, he has to out-smart being caught by fishermen and his fellow lobsters, as both are carnivorous by nature.

First Lobster Hatchery

The Lobster Hatchery at Padstow in North Cornwall was set up in the year 2000. The project's aim is to return a larger number of young lobsters to the sea; in the wild just one in ten thousand eggs would survive to maturity. To date the hatchery has released 38,000 lobsters and hopes to increase that number during the coming years.

Oldest Pilchard Processor

Tolcarne, Newlyn is the home of the last UK producer of the traditional salted pilchard, and although at the time of writing a quantity of the original product remains available; when it's gone it's gone and at present no one can say when it will return. The pilchard works, which for the last ten years operated as a working museum finally closed its doors to the public in October 2005, due to a decline in orders as salted pilchards fell from favour. Cornish pilchards had been exported to the Mediterranean since 1550 and the Tolcarne works had supplied four generations of one Italian family business, over a period of over one hundred years. However, all is not lost as the humble pilchard or sardine, as indeed they are one and the same is now available in vacuum packs, they can also be prepared to requirements by the Newlyn based company which is still operating. Freshly landed Cornish pilchards are dispatched by the oldest pilchard processor in Cornwall, to the oldest family run sardine cannery in Brittany, where they are specially prepared and placed in cans bearing a print of Cornish fisher-folk, by Walter Langley, a member of the Newlyn School of Artists.

Cornish tinned Pilchards

Largest fleet

Newlyn has England's largest fishing fleet. In the year 2005, 7,500 tons of wet fish were landed valued at £17.5 million. At any one time the port handles over forty species of fish, i.e. Monk, Megrim, Pollock, Hake, Ling, Sole, Lemon Sole, Sardines, Turbot, Mackerel, John Dory, Red Mullet, Bass, Cuttlefish, Squid and Ray. They also land Crabs, Lobsters, Crawfish and Scallops.

Largest Catch

In the 19th century St Ives was the centre of the Seine net fishing for pilchards and in 1834 possibly the largest catch ever; 30 million pilchards were enclosed in one net in one hour. By 1907 the catches were around 24 million in one year and this marked the decline in the pilchard industry. Up until that point, the coastal fishing villages were heavily involved harvesting the vast shoals that filled the waters of the West.

Earliest Farmers

Cornwall was at the fore front of man's early attempts at agriculture. The earliest evidence of this was to be found at Carn Brea around 3700 and 3400 BC. Evidence suggests that the community was harmonious and all food produced was evenly distributed. It was not until they achieved success with an abundance of crops which were harvested and set aside for winter, that friction set in, leading to battles with neighbouring groups who came to pillage.

First British Asparagus

Cornish farmer Mark Rowe of Pentire Farm Helston has won the unofficial race to deliver the first British asparagus of 2007. March 19th was the record breaking date when this early spring vegetable was delivered to major supermarkets throughout the UK. Many local shops, hotels and restaurants have also benefited from the exceptionally early crop.

Earliest Potatoes

Approximately five-hundred hectares of land is used for the production of Cornwall's famous early potato crop. The crop is harvested and available to the consumer from the third week in April.

Cornish Potatos

Largest Witness

In November 1941 a large and unusual witness was called to end a long running dispute between two neighbouring farmers. The two farmers each claimed to be the owner of the same cow; a heifer called Jenny. In the bitter court case that followed at Camelford County Court the Judge decided to allow Jenny to decide who her rightful owner was. Adjourning the case, they proceeded to a smallholding owned by one of the farmers. Each was instructed to stand either side of the cow to see which one Jenny favoured. The cow, without any prompting ambled towards one of the farmer's cowmen and after nuzzling him, raised her body aloft and rested her front legs upon his shoulders. The dispute was brought to a swift end and Jenny was reunited with her rightful owner.

FARMING

Biggest Cheese

Davidstow cheese has been produced in the county for over fifty years. The cheese, a type of Cheddar is currently consumed by 3.8 million households. Its consistent performance has been rewarded on many occasions in special cheese shows across the UK.

Largest Independent Creamery

For over a century from Rodda's creamery at Scorrier has been the largest independent producer of Cornish clotted cream using milk from Cornish farms. No Cornish cream tea would be possible without this delicious treat. It is enjoyed by both royalty and prime ministers; one of whom, Lord Gladstone, declared that clotted cream was the food of Gods.

First Friesians

The first herd of Friesian cows was introduced into the county in the 1920's. Alfred Browning Lyne, founder of the Cornish Guardian whose hobby was farming, made a special journey up country to get them.

Smallest Fields

Near Lamorna in the west of the region, evidence still remains of small enclosed fields, which were used to grow violets. Some of the fields were no larger than ten foot by twelve foot square. To augment their income, families cultivated violets to meet the demand by the fashionable wealthy in London. The coming of the railways facilitated the speedy transportation to London, making violets a lucrative crop. It took two and a half hours to pick and bunch a boxful of the flowers which were then sent to market. A box could fetch as much as fifteen pounds.

Largest Grower of Daffodil Bulbs

The mild climate enables Cornwall to be the largest grower of daffodil bulbs in the world. The land allocated is 2,123 hectares producing 64,000 tons of bulbs per season. Half of these are kept back for planting after two years.

Daffodil Field

Largest Producer of Tin

Until the end of the 20th century Cornwall was the world's biggest producer of tin and copper. A quantity of lead, arsenic, mundic and even silver being amongst the by-products.

Cornish Tin Mine headgear

Earliest Bal Maidens

The earliest reference to bal maidens in Cornwall was at the Bere Alston mines at Calstock on the Tamar River in May 1306. A bal maiden was a female surface worker employed in breaking and washing lead and silver ore. Breaking and sorting ore with hammers and hand tools in the open air could hardly be said to be the answer to a maiden's prayer. The job was hard and dirty but it gave the women a freedom to work in a male environment at a time when females were not fully emancipated.

Only Female Mine Manager

Magdalen Mine at Ponsanooth first mentioned in 1522 was named after a nearby Chantry Chapel dedicated to St Mary Magdalen. The mine employed the only female mine manager in Cornwall; perhaps an early recognition of the ability of woman power in the workplace.

Greatest Industrial Work

The Great County Adit was an enormous industrial undertaking for its time. Started in 1748 by John Williams of Scorrier; manager of the Poldice Mine. The adit was an underground tunnel designed as a mining drainage system. Thirty eight miles in length, and a hundred fathoms deep in places; at its peak the adit drained thirteen million gallons of water a day from over forty mines.

Earliest Mention

The earliest written mention of the Cornish tin industry was in circa 325 BC by Pytheas of Massalia, and his writings were later quoted by Diodorus Siculus in the first century BC.

First Steam Engine

In September 1777 a 30 inch cylinder engine designed by James Watt was erected at Wheal Busy. It was a low pressure steam engine and its innovative use doubled the efficiency and economy. James Watt was of the opinion that Richard Trevithick and his fellow Cornish engineers were reckless and their inventions fraught with danger. Being independently minded, the Cornish disregarded the Scotsman's opinion; after all he was from over the Tamar. The Trevithick engine, which was high pressured steam went on to be used successfully.

Largest Beam Engine

The largest Cornish beam engine, having a 100 inch diameter cylinder engine, was in use at East Wheal Rose.

First Stannary Charter

King John issued the first Cornish Stannary Charter in 1201. The term stannary means one or more tin mining districts throughout the county. Cornwall was divided into four districts and within these the crown designated certain towns to be coinage towns. All tin had to be taken to these centres for assaying before it could be sold. The tin ingot would be weighed and coined, this process involved removing a small corner from the ingot which would then be analysed for impurities. This procedure took place four times a year.

First Gunpowder Use

In the summer of 1689 the Great Work Mine at Germoe was the first mine to use gunpowder for shot-hole blasting.

Greatest Depth

Dolcoath, at over 3,100 feet is the deepest mine in the county. This mine has the deepest vertical shaft at about 3,096 feet from collar to sump. It boasts the deepest shaft (New Sump Shaft) which is over 3,500 feet deep, it is not vertical but follows the dip of the load-: 3,500 feet between adit (180feet) and the 550fathom level, and then goes more than 100feet below that level.

Greatest Disaster

East Wheal Rose, a lead mine, was the scene of the greatest loss of life. It was flooded by a cloud burst in July 1846 resulting in the death by drowning of thirty-nine men and boys. Thirty-one men and boys lost their lives in the Levant Mine disaster of 1919 when the bolts sheared off causing the collapse of the Man Engine.

UK's First World Surfing Championship

The UK's first World Surfing Championships took place at Fistral Beach Newquay in 1994. More than 1500 competitors took part; a fitting venue as this beach is regarded as the home of British surfing.

First Kneeboard Championship

Fistral Beach saw the first ever Kneeboard Championships in Britain in 2003.

S.A.S.

Not to be confused with the Special Air Service, Surfers Against Sewage is successfully fighting its own long standing campaign. The pressure group was formed in 1990 and has done much to promote public awareness regarding the millions of tonnes of waste polluting our waters.

First Surfing Degree Course

Such is the interest in Surfing today that some forty-five years on from its early beginnings, the first University Degree Course, Surf Science and Technology is now available through Cornwall College. The beach based course at Lusty Glaze runs for two years covering sport, business, product design and hydrodynamic engineering etc with graduates expected to take jobs in this now flourishing industry.

Surfing First

Martin Potter who honed his surfing skills at Newquay was World Surfing Champion in 1989.

Greatest Influence

British born Rod Sumpter returned to the UK in 1966, having been brought up in Australia. By the time of his arrival Rod was already Australian Junior Champion and had won the US Junior Championships in California. He brought with him a style and professionalism that was new to the Cornish surfing scene. Rod mesmerized onlookers at Watergate and Tolcarne beaches with his technique; becoming a figure that the young surfers all tried to emulate. He had a major impact on board development and surfing in general.

A Surfer

Only Cornish Capped Cricketer

John Frederick Crapp born at St Columb Major on 14th October 1912 was the first Cornishman to play for England. His first Test appearance was in the England v Australia 3rd test at Old Trafford in 1948. Jack was the only Cornishman up until 1984 to wear an England Cap.

Jack Crapps MCC jacket etc. is now housed in the library at St Columb Major; it used to be on display in the post office for many years.

Smallest Football League

The Isles of Scilly is home to the smallest football league in England. The league is made up of two teams; the Garrison Gunners and the Woolpack Wanderers; the players are drawn from the surrounding islands. Their shared home ground is the Garrison field on St Mary's.

Only Boxer

The only Briton to hold the title, Heavyweight Champion of the World was Bob Fitzsimons, born in Helston in 1863. Having arrived in America as a young man he went on to become a legend in his lifetime. He was the first boxer to win three world titles; Middleweight in 1891, Heavyweight in 1897, which was regarded as the fight of the century and was witnessed by famous characters of the time including Wyatt Earp. He won his last title; Light-Heavyweight at the age of 41 in 1903. He led a colourful life which matched his nickname of Ruby Robert. He appeared on Broadway, kept exotic animals and ended his days as an evangelist.

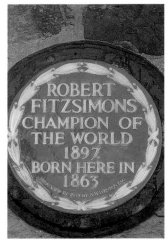

Bob Fitzsimons Plaque

Great Writers

It is impossible to mention all the writers associated with Cornwall many of whom are noteworthy. We have selected a few names for inclusion. Cornish born Rosamund Pilcher, famous for her novel and TV dramas Coming Home and Winter Solstice. E V Thompson, writer of the Retallick sagas. D M Thomas, who wrote an international best seller, The White Hotel and a biography of Alexander Solzhenitsyn. Cornishman Jack Clemo, the clay pit poet. J C Trewin, journalist and theatre critic who wrote Up From The Lizard and The Edwardian Theatre. Sir John Betjeman and DH Lawrence. Maria Branwell, mother of the famous Bronte sisters, Charlotte, Emily and Anne was born in Penzance 1783. Charles Kingsley attended Helston Grammar School, then known as the Eton of the West. We could go on and on.

William Golding

Cornish Novelist and Poet. William Golding (1911-1993) was born in Cornwall at St Columb Minor. He was awarded the Booker Prize in 1980 for his book 'Rites of Passage' which was part of a trilogy; followed by the Nobel Prize for Literature in 1983. He is probably best known for his book 'Lord of the Flies' which he wrote in 1954. Golding received a knighthood in 1988.

Winston Graham

Eighteenth century industrial Cornwall was magically brought to life through the eyes of Winston Graham's Poldark series of 12 books. The books became so popular, that some were eventually dramatised for television and distributed to networks world wide. Winston Graham was a Fellow of the Royal Society of Literature and was awarded the O.B.E in 1983.

A L Rowse

Born December 1903 at St Austell into a working class family where home stimulus was lacking, Rowse went on to become an outstanding scholar. In 1921 aged seventeen he went up to Oxford, attending Christ Church College where he read English, later turning to History. At the age of twenty three he was made a Fellow of All Souls; the first person from a working class background to join this elite group. He is credited with identifying Shakespeare's dark lady of the Sonnets. He died in 1997.

Arthur Quiller Couch 'Q'

Author and Historian Arthur Quiller Couch was born in Bodmin in 1863 and went on to attend Trinity College Oxford where he later became a lecturer. His book Troy Town which he wrote in 1888 was based on the town of Fowey. He was knighted in 1910 and became a Professor of English Literature at Cambridge.

Daphne du Maurier

One only need mention her name and immediately Cornwall springs to mind, followed by the images of wind swept moors, secluded creeks, cliff top mansions and out of the way villages. Her books such as Jamaica Inn, Frenchman's Creek and Rebecca have done much to encourage her readers to visit Cornwall and soak up the atmosphere evoked by her novels. The fame of her work has spawned the Festival of Arts and Literature which is held at Fowey in May of each year.

John Le Carre

Master of the spy novel and crime thriller; John Le Carre has spent many years living in Cornwall. He wrote the novel 'The Spy That Came In From The Cold', drawing on his experiences from the time spent as a spy for the British Foreign Service.

Virginia Woolf

Cornwall had a powerful and life long place in the imagination of the novelist Virginia Woolf (1882-1941). The summers of her earliest years were spent at Talland House above Porthminster Beach, St Ives. Her fifth novel written in 1927, 'To the Lighthouse', was inspired by the flora and fauna which is indigenous to Cornwall as well as the people and landscape. Godrevy Lighthouse in St Ives Bay became the main focus for her book. She set the story however, on the Isle of Skye where the animals and plants differed to that of Cornwall. She received many letters from Scots who pointed out the inaccuracies. Nevertheless the book has become a classic in English literature.

Godrevy Lighthouse

Charles Causley

Cornwall's Poet Laureate. Described as one of the most important poets of his day, Charles Causley produced a large body of work. His first poetry collection 'Farewell Aggie Weston' was published in 1951. He was born in Launceston in 1917 where he lived and taught in a primary school there for most of his life. He received many awards, the Queens Medal for Poetry in 1967, was made a CBE in 1986 and a Companion of Literature by the Royal Society of Literature at the age of 83 years. He was much respected by his fellow poets. This modest man, who remained young at heart and displayed a touch of the rebel in his work died at the age of 86 years in 2003.

Great Film Locations

Film makers have used Cornwall since the 1920's; its temperate climate and dramatic scenery lends itself to the varied genres. Here we have highlighted just a few of the many films made in the county.

Saving Grace 2000

Newly widowed Grace, played by Brenda Blethyn finds herself in dire financial straits. With the aid of her gardener she finds a creative but criminal way of alleviating her circumstances. The British Government had to grant permission for the use of the real Pot plant props and these were guarded throughout the filming. Port Isaac and Boscastle are just two of the places used for filming. Leslie Phillips, Diana Quick and Martin Clunes co-starred.

Mullion Harbour

Never Let Me Go 1953

This film brought Hollywood heart throb Clark Gable to the sleepy shores of Cornwall, sending shockwaves throughout the female population; many of whom would have gladly swapped places with leading lady Gene Tierney. Scenes for this romantic movie were shot at Mullion harbour, Newquay and Mevagissey.

The Witches 1988

A Roald Dahl scary, where a little boy gets turned into a mouse after discovering a witches' convention whilst on a sea-side holiday. Newquay's Headland Hotel was the venue and Anjelica Huston, is a convincing chief witch. Other members of the cast included Rowan Atkinson, Brenda Blethyn and Jane Horrocks.

Ladies in Lavender 2004

Charles Dance as director brought the grand Dames of stage and screen to Cornwall. Filming took place at Cadgwith, Helston and Penzance featuring Dames Judi Dench and Maggie Smith. The film included a fine performance by Miriam Margolyes; even the locals had a part to play. The story revolves around a young man washed up on the beach and the emotions his arrival evokes in their lives.

Cadgwith

Straw Dogs 1971

This controversial film entered the debate about depicting unacceptable levels of screen violence. Set in St Buryan and Lamorna Cove it starred Dustin Hoffman and Susan George.

Love Story 1944

This emotionally charged film starring Stewart Granger, Margaret Lockwood and Patricia Roc gave birth to the piece of music known as the Cornish Rhapsody. The Minack Theatre at Porthcurno was the dramatic setting for the film.

Magical Mystery Tour 1967

Newquay's Atlantic Hotel, Towan Beach and Bodmin featured in this film which brought the Beatles to Cornwall. Considered somewhat bizarre and fragmented when made; today it is viewed as being ahead of its time and has a cult following.

The Eagle Has Landed 1976

Based on a book by Jack Higgins this Second World War thriller centred on a plot to kidnap Winston Churchill. In spite of its all star cast including Michael Caine, Donald Sutherland, Robert Duval and Donald Pleasance it failed to thrill. Filmed on location at RAF St Mawgan and Charlestown.

Hwerow Hweg 2001

This modern love story was filmed entirely on location in the county and is the first feature film to be shot in both the English and Cornish languages; the English version being one minute thirty seconds longer. Hungarian, Antal Kovacs wrote and directed the film having made Cornwall his spiritual home, and it was he who harnessed the talents of local actors and technicians. The film has the added distinction of having had its world premiere at the House of Commons.

First Rail

Though not classed as a railway as such, the Poldice to Portreath Tramroad was very important in the transportation of ore extracted from the Cornish mines. On the 25th October 1809 the first rail was laid at Portreath. This significant step was intended to make the transportation of large quantities of copper and tin much easier. The rail network was laid in sections which incorporated the heavily industrialised mining districts of Scorrier and St Day. The whole track was completed in 1819 linking the harbour at Portreath to the harbour at Devoran on the opposite coast. As a result of mining closures the tracks were removed, but in recent times the tramroad has become popular cycle routes.

Largest Viaduct

Wealthy landowner, Joseph Thomas Treffry was responsible for the building of the large granite viaduct which spans the Luxulyan Valley. The giant structure was built between 1839 and 1842 measuring 648 feet (approx 200m) long and 98 feet (approx 30.15m high), it also served as an aqueduct.. It is considered one of the seven wonders of the west country.

Treffry Viaduct

Longest Tunnel

The longest railway tunnel in the county of Cornwall is to be found at St Pinnock near Fowey and stretches approximately 1,173 yards. It is now abandoned.

First Diesel Train

The county of Cornwall was chosen to be one of the first areas in the country to be dieselised; 1958 saw the first diesel hauled train.

First Passenger Railway

The Hayle railway, although primarily a mineral transport route for Camborne and Redruth mines and taking in the ports of Hayle and Portreath, became the first passenger carrying railway in West Cornwall in 1837.

Brunel's Greatest Structure

The railway bridge linking Cornwall to Devon is The Royal Albert Bridge, which crosses the River Tamar at Saltash to Plymouth. It was constructed at a cost of £225,000 and is 2,200 feet long and 100 feet above the water. Designed by Isambard Kingdom Brunel, the bridge was completed in 1859 and opened by Prince Albert; the year of Brunel's death.

Greatest Gesture

The newly formed Great Western Railway had a policy of allowing coffins to be transported free of charge. Entrepreneurial Cornish daffodil growers spotted this as an economic opportunity, if somewhat devious way of getting their produce to wholesalers throughout the country, and it was by this means that many fragrant filled caskets reached their destinations.

Great Western Railway

Cornwall had a network of independent railways until the turn of the 20th century when they were gradually absorbed by the GWR into a combined network. This enabled farmers and flower growers to reach lucrative markets beyond Cornwall and was a boost to the economy of the county.

Royal Albert Bridge

First Layered Road

In 1798 John McAdam who came to Cornwall as a Navy Victualling Officer was the first to recognise the merit of Cornish Greenstone as a base for new roads. From his work in Cornwall we have the word Macadam Road.

First Summer Gritters

In July 2006 winter gritters were called out to scatter sand and gravel on some of the county's roads. Temperatures had soared above thirty degrees centigrade causing road surfaces to melt.

Smallest Alley

Squeeze-ee-Belly Alley in Port Isaac is not so much a road rather a walkway. It measures just nineteen and a half inches across and is the narrowest of such alley-ways qualifying it for The Guinness Book of Records.

First Macadam Road

The earliest use of McAdam's material was on the turnpike road from Truro Workhouse to Kiggion, now part of the A39.

Sqeeze-ee-Belly Alley

Road Statistics

	Miles	Kilometres
Trunk Road-Single carriageway (inc. slip roads)	65	105
Trunk Road-Dual carriageway	50	81
Trunk Road-Total	115	186
Classified Principal (A-class, non Trunk)	346	557
Classified Numbered (B class)	360	580
Classified Un-numbered (C class)	1639	2637
Unclassified	2185	3517
Total Road Length	4646	7478
Bridleways, Footpaths and Byways	2715	4369
Personal injury accidents	2057	

As of 1st April 2004

Most Expensive Road

The long awaited and much needed Bodmin to Indian Queens bypass is 11.57 km, or 7 miles long. The cost of the work is £93 million which works out at £13.285 million per mile. A £500,000 archeological survey was carried out by means of a ten metre wide trench down the entire length of the site. Remains of a henge circle and also a roundhouse were among the discoveries made.

Oldest English Oak Tree

The Tree Council, a conservation charity, selected fifty great British trees, varying from the oldest to the rarest to mark the Golden Jubilee of Queen Elizabeth II. One of these trees is the Darley Oak at Upton Cross, near Liskeard believed to be around one thousand years old. The owners of the chosen trees were issued with certificates and commemorative plaques.

Oldest Mulberry Tree

In the far south of Cornwall on a private Estate stands the largest and oldest Mulberry tree in the country. It is mentioned in the Great Domesday Survey of 1086. (Exeter Roll) Mulberry trees were introduced for the domestic silk industry. Unfortunately this particular tree is a black mulberry; not suitable for the silk worm which prefers the white mulberry.

The Darley Oak

Earliest Plant Hunters

Amongst the early plant hunters were brothers William and Thomas Lobb; both were prolific plant hunters. In November 1840 at the age of thirty-one William left Falmouth and sailed on his first plant hunting expedition to Brazil, the Andes and Chile. He is synonymous with introducing the Auracaria Auracana (Monkey Puzzle Tree) from Chile and the massive Sequoiadendron giganteum into Great Britain from North America.

Rare Plants

The Lizard is an area of particular interest to botanists, being the habitat to plants found nowhere else in Britain. Many are plain and unassuming, but nevertheless are gems in their own right. Some to look out for are the 'Land Quillwort' which appears in April, the 'Fringed Rupturewort' and the serpentine loving 'Cornish Heath'.

Largest National Garden Museum

Trevarno House and Gardens near Helston has the largest collection of garden memorabilia in the country. There are ten designated areas each assigned to various aspects of gardening, including gardening exhibits from the 17th and 18th centuries. These include purpose made tools and exhibits such as seed catalogues and rosettes won by local gardeners. The museum achieved National status in 2001.

Earliest Nursery Growers

Tresidders Nursery was run by five generations of this family from the mid 1830's. They were the leading nurserymen in Cornwall and the first to produce and sell their products commercially; being the forerunners of present day garden centres.

.

First Tea Plantation

A recent development in plant life in Cornwall is the now up and running tea plantation at Tregothnan Estate Truro; the first truly English tea has been successfully produced. It has been developed using a special form of Camellia sinensis and the tea is now available commercially.

Tregothnan Tea

First Discovery of New Species

Known as Phytophthora Ramorum, this pathogen first found in European nurseries in the early nineties was subsequently found to be present in the UK by 2002. During surveys by tree pathologist Professor Clive Brasier and his colleagues at Forest Research, a new species of the pathogen Phytophthora was discovered in a Cornish woodland. To distinguish this new species it was given the name Phytophthora Kernoviae; the latter part of the name meaning Cornwall. This invasive pathogen causes bleeding stem legions on forest trees and foliar necrosis of ornamentals in the UK. It is thought that the transportation of plants globally has contributed to the spread of the disease.

Only Bird Sanctuary

Mousehole Bird Sanctuary and Hospital was founded in 1928 by sisters Dorothy and Phyllis Yglesias. During the Torrey Canyon Disaster of 1967 the resulting oil slick from the wrecked ship not only polluted the coastline but drastically affected the wildlife. The hospital was a lifesaver to many of the 8,000 sea birds that were brought to it. The good work continues to this day and has done much to extend the lives of native wild birds and sea birds. The sanctuary is run purely by voluntary contributions.

Only Place

The Lesser White Toothed Shrew can be found on the Isles of Scilly, but this continental shrew is absent from mainland Britain.

Wildlife Veterinary Investigation Centre

The WVIC was officially opened in August 2001. It was established by veterinary pathologist Vic Simpson and it is the first and only wildlife pathology lab in the United Kingdom. Tucked away in a quiet backwater near Chacewater Cornwall, this vital research has enabled the centre to ensure the long term welfare of all wildlife species including otters and swans.

First and Largest Seal Sanctuary

Nestling at the head of the Helford River is Gweek; home to the National Seal Sanctuary. The 40 acre site has a fully equipped hospital and ten outdoor pools. The sanctuary rescues on average more than thirty seals per year and where possible, releases them back into the wild; less able bodied animals take residence and are cared for indefinitely.

Large Butterfly comes back

Once commonly found in Cornwall, the 'Large Blue' butterfly, Maculinea arion became extinct in 1975. This butterfly depends on thyme flowers and the ant, Myrmica sabuleti for its survival. The ant in turn can only survive in turf less than 2 cm on warm south facing slopes, and it was the loss of this habitat through changes in farming that led to the Large Blue's demise. Much scientific work has been carried out and a suitable habitat recreated with the successful re-introduction in 2000.

First Cornish Choughs in Fifty Years

A member of the crow family, the Cornish chough has always been synonymous with Cornwall and it is even featured on the county's coat of arms. The decline of this raven-like bird with its distinctive curved red bill and red legs had been attributed to its loss of feeding ground as a result of intensive farming. However, for the first time in fifty years a pair of wild choughs has successfully nested on the cliff tops of Cornwall and the numbers are steadily growing.

Cornwall's Landscape has many diverse habitats

Rare Snow in Cornwall

Coldest Inland Temperature

Bastreet, Bodmin Moor, recorded a temperature of minus 15°C on 1st January 1979.

Coldest Coastal Temperature

The influence of the sea usually prevents the coastal regions and Isles of Scilly from extreme low temperatures, except when a strong cold easterly wind ousts the normal south-westerlies. Such an occasion was on the 13th January 1987, which was reputed to be the coldest day of the 20th century in the South West. On that day minima of -9°C was recorded at St Mawgan and -6.4°C on the Isles of Scilly.

The Wettest Place

Taking the averages over a 30 year period, the highest value of rainfall is recorded at Cardinham near Bodmin, which qualifies it as the wettest place in Cornwall with an annual mean 1387.14 mm. No doubt the rainfall helped create the moor-land heath and beautiful wooded valleys in this district, which covers some nine thousand acres.

Sea Temperatures

Cornwall has the highest sea temperatures in the whole of Britain, especially in winter; sea temperatures are warmer in September and October than in May and June. The temperature builds up during the summer months and retains its warmth until around February and March, by then it has reached its lowest temperature.

Greatest Blizzard

Havoc was wreaked across the British Isles in the spring of 1891. Even Cornwall with its moderate climate felt the wrath of the blizzards, with snow drifting up to twenty feet. The hurricane force winds brought destruction to more than half a million trees and 200 people lost their lives; most at sea as 63 ships foundered. More than 6,000 sheep and lambs died; Mevagissey's outer harbour was washed away and vital telegraph lines linking Porthcurno to Penzance were damaged as a result of heavy snow.

Sunshine

The actual hours of sunshine for Cornwall in 2005 were 620.6: coming second to those attained by the south east which reached 658.7.

Flooding at Boscastle

On the 16th August 2004 the inhabitants of Boscastle witnessed an unprecedented freak weather storm. The serious nature of the floods was caused by thundery showers and strong coastal winds which had built up during the day. The topography of the area contributed to the resulting deluge. In spite of the severity, thankfully no lives were lost.

Hottest Month

The hottest month recorded was June 1976, when the temperature reached 33.9°C at Ellbridge in Cornwall.

Highest Gust

The highest gust of wind recorded at a low level site was 103knots (118 mph) at Gwennap Head in Cornwall on December 15th 1979.

First Railway Trip

Thomas Cook was the first to organise a holiday railway trip across Brunel's Royal Albert Bridge over the River Tamar in 1859, within six weeks of its opening. Since that time Cornwall has become more and more popular as a holiday resort resulting in a large proportion of business's catering for the tourist industry. The seasonal influx of visitors provides services which allow small businesses to flourish. Current figures state that 87.5% of visitors travelled to the county by car, 5.4% by coach, 4.2% by train and 2.9% by air and other modes.

Tourist Pioneer

Sylvanus Trevail, Cornwall's leading architect and developer saw the potential of tourism with the advent of the railways in the 19th century. He was instrumental in designing and constructing The Atlantic and Headland Hotels in Newquay. Not everyone shared his enthusiasm, least of all the outraged farmers and fishermen; a riot ensued whereby buildings were torn down and materials were hurled over the cliff. The hotels were eventually built and the tide of tourism has flowed ever since.

The Headland Hotel

Great Cultural Interest

With increasing interest in our archaeological sites representing every period of history, from the magical Tintagel Castle, ancient Standing Stones and the bronze age village of Chysauster, to the success of modern day attractions, such as The Eden Project, which alone is estimated to have generated £450 million pounds for the local economy, and the now established Tate St Ives, along with The National Maritime Museum Falmouth, Cornwall has been able to extend its season.

World Heritage Site

The historic mining area of Cornwall is recognised by UNESCO as a World Heritage Site, one of only 30 in the whole of the UK. This puts a selected group of the Cornish landscape on a level with Stonehenge and the Taj Mahal.

Chysauster

First Man over Niagara Falls

On July 19th 1911 Cornishman Bobby Leach (born 1858) took the plunge. He was the first man to go over The Horseshoe Falls at Niagara in a steel barrel and live to tell the tale. But as a result of his dare-devil escapade, Bobby spent several months in hospital recuperating from his injuries. Ironically, many years later at the age of 67 he slipped on orange peel while walking on a street in New Zealand; after developing complications, sadly, Bobby died from gangrene poisoning.

Oldest Manmade Structures

Cornwall's bronze-age field boundaries and hedges are the oldest man built structures still in every day use. They provide an excellent highway for animals and creatures to move freely around the county.

Largest Treasure Trove

Forty miles off the Cornish coast, in May of 2007, Odyssey Marine Exploration from the USA discovered the wreck of a ship believed to be the 17th century Dartmouth based ship, called the Merchant Royal, which sank in 1641. Using a tethered underwater robot the team found half a million silver and gold coins, which were in mint condition. The estimated value is £253 million or $500 million. The treasure has all gone to the USA as the ship was located in international waters.

Greatest Benefactor

John Passmore Edwards was born in Blackwater of humble birth in 1823. He became a journalist and went on to become editor of a major London newspaper and an MP for Salisbury. Renowned as an outstanding philanthropist and champion of the working classes, he established through his bequests and gifts many buildings such as libraries, hospitals, schools, convalescent homes and art galleries, both in Cornwall and other parts of the country to improve social progress for all.

Passmore Edwards building

Greatest Rescue

The sea at Britain's most Southerly point, The Lizard has claimed its share of shipwrecks. The 'SS Suevic' might have suffered a similar fate had it not been for the heroic efforts of the volunteers who man our lifeboats. The White Star Liner 'Suevic' homeward bound from Australia ran on to the Maenheere Reef in fog and stormy seas. All the lifeboats in the area were called, The Lizard, Cadgwith, Coverack and Porthleven and they succeeded in rescuing everyone, a total of 524 passengers and crew. This is the greatest number ever rescued in the history of The Royal National Lifeboat Institution. The R.N.L.I awarded six silver medals to those who were instrumental in the rescue. Considering this rescue occurred some hundred years ago on 17th March 1907 using man power only, open boats and oars; it was a truly extraordinary feat.

First Supplier of Rum

Lemon Hart Rum, which is still available today, was first produced by a Cornishman who opened his wine and spirits business from cellars in Penzance in 1804. Mr Lehmynn or Lemon Hart as he became known managed to secure the first contract to supply the Royal Navy with rum. His blend is sourced from Jamaica, Trinidad, Barbados and Demerara, now Guyana. It preceded the later "dark" rum which became available in the mid nineteenth century.

Lemon Hart Rum

Rare Sturgeon

When Jon Tonkin caught a 6ft sturgeon off the coast of Cadgwith in April 2001, the fish was offered to the Duke of Cornwall. It was 2 metres long and weighed 46 kg (101 lb). It was eventually served up in a Bath restaurant. Sturgeon caught anywhere else within 3 miles of the British coast, is offered to the monarch. This tradition dates back to the reign of Edward II (1307-1327). Queen Elizabeth II favours the continuation of this tradition. The last sturgeon to be eaten at Buckingham Palace was in 1969.

First Space Tourists

Sir Richard Branson is considering Newquay as a possible launching site when he starts his Space Tourism flights. Could this be another first for Cornwall? But that as they say, is in the future!!!

The population at the last Census in 2001 was 501,267 an increase of 7% in ten years. There are 242,487 males and 258,780 females

4,500 are over the age of 90

27% of households have no car
1.4% have 4 or more cars

There are 373 people per square mile
3369 people declared themselves as Jedi at the last census.

(Remember, it was the MP for Helston, Cornwall who introduced the first census. Helston's current population is 9,780.)

The area of Cornwall is 356,265 hectares or 1376 square miles.
The total Agricultural Area is 279,962 hectares

Cornwall is one of the poorest and most deprived areas of the UK with a GVA per head of 65% of the national average and a GDP per head just 2/3rds of the national figure.

Acknowlegements

Mining. Allen Buckley M Phil, BA, FRHistS.

Meteorological Office. Graham Bartlett, Library Information Manager.

Redruth History Centre.

Angela Broome, Librarian Archivist, Courtney Library, Royal Institution of Cornwall.

Gaia Energy Centre.

Ellen McConnell Manager Wheal Martyn St Austell.

Cornwall County Council Website.

Delank Quarry, Mr David Methven.

Fishing. John Lansley, Office Manager of Cornish Fishing resource centre.

Animal Life. Vic Simpson.BVSc, DTVM, CBiol,

FIBiol, Hon. FRCVS Pathologist WVIC Chacewater

Mousehole Bird Sanctuary

Plant Life. Professor Clive Brassier & Team at Forest Research, Farnham & Gordon Hanks Senior Research Scientist, Warwick HRI & DEFFRA Advisor

Coastguard Press Officer Richard Skeats

Books.

Curiosities of Cornwall by Margaret Caine & Alan Gorton
A History of Cornwall by Ian Soulsby
Old Penzance by A. Edgar Reece.
Cornwall's Railways by Tony Fairclough
A History of Jamaica Inn by Rose Mullins
Marconi at The Lizard by Courtney Rowe, MBE BSc
U Boat Hunters
Cornwall's Air War 1916-1919 by Peter London

Special thanks to our respective husbands, Richard for the constant supply of delicious coffee and technical support and David for his patience and understanding.